SIMPLY DIGITAL

*A Jargon-Free Small Business
Survival Guide To The Digital World*

Brandon Tidd

Printed by CreateSpace
Edited by Carol H. Schroeder

Dedication

This book is dedicated first and foremost to my wife Shirah. Without her support, as well as the support of my family and friends, I would not be where I am today. I have also been privileged to be mentored by two influential thought-leaders throughout my career: Vince Ing and Dave Baumgartner. Finally, this book would never have been published if not for the motivational energy and efforts of Hal Elrod, author of *"The Miracle Morning,"* Chandler Bolt, author of *"Book Launch,"* and Amy Neumann, author of *"Uplifting Quotes on Gratitude and Goodness to Show Appreciation."* They all led by example and paved the way for my future success.

Contents

Forward

25 Action Item Review

Forward

I still remember the first time I was introduced to the Internet. I had walked into the library that day with the intention of simply returning a book that I had borrowed. Suddenly, a computer workstation from across the room caught my eye. A blue sign inviting library guests to try the 'new' Internet hung welcomingly from the ceiling. The soft glow from the monitor beckoned, masking the hidden treasures of a new world behind a curtain of never-ending stars. Curiosity piqued, I cautiously sat down and gave the mouse a gentle tug. On command the screen immediately sprang to life, presenting me with an array of categories to choose from. News, weather, entertainment, stocks... a world of information was now just a couple of clicks away.

The Internet has come a long way from its humble beginnings. It has so deeply penetrated our culture that we no longer search for information, we "Google it." In fact, according to research from Harvard University and the University of Colorado at Boulder, the Internet (and its 'human' translator, Siri) is literally changing the way our brains retain information.

"The distinction between the internal and the external—what resides in our minds as opposed to what a friend knows—changes radically when the confidant is the Internet. The information retrieved from the Internet now arrives sometimes more quickly than what we can pull out of our own memories. The immediacy with which a search result pops onto the screen of a Smartphone may start to blur the boundaries between our personal memories and the vast digital troves distributed across the Internet." [1]

This shift not only has broad implications for how we live our lives, but also directly impacts the ways in which we expect to conduct business. The slow and sometimes painful transition away from "the way things were" is nearly complete. Tried and true methodologies are less relevant than ever, and small business owners are left to pick up the pieces.

---

[1] *Scientific American "The Internet Has Become The External Hard Drive For Our Memories," Daniel M. Wegner & Adrian F. Ward, November 19, 2013*

What you won't find in this book: Technospeak.[2]   There are a number of resources dedicated to defining the Internet. As with anything new, the concepts illustrated within these pages will take some time to be absorbed and accepted. With a willingness to keep an open mind, however, I think you will find this to be an informative and comfortable conversation that covers the most frequent concepts that the average small business owner encounters.

I invite you to join me on this journey of digital exploration. It is my hope that this book will serve as a roadmap to help you navigate the new world. I'm not going to make you an overnight expert. Rather, this guide should serve as a foundation of knowledge from which to expand upon as you find necessary. The fact that you are reading this book tells me that you are already interested. Don't stop now, we're just getting started!

~ Brandon Tidd

---

[2] *Not a technical term.*

Chapter 1
The New Normal

"If Nothing Ever Changed, There Would Be No Butterflies." - Author Unknown

Back in the days when AOL was still overwhelming your mail carrier with CDs offering '100 free hours' of the Internet, having a website meant you were an industry leader regardless of what industry you were in. You knew your business, and as long as you also knew someone who had a basic knowledge of how to build a website your digital needs were met. Early forms of social media and 'smart' technology existed, but not even the most prevalent 'early adopters' of these platforms expected much from them.

When Apple debuted the first generation iPhone in 2007, they disrupted **twenty-seven** industries[3] (including, but not limited to, calculator and flashlight sales). Since then, humans have been on a fast-track collision course with technology. In less than a decade, mobile devices such as Smartphones and

---

[3] *R. "Ray" Wang, author of "Disrupting Digital Business."*

tablets like the iPad overtook traditional desktop and laptop Internet use. In fact, according to the industry leading technology measurement company comScore, as of mid-2014 60% of all online use originated from one of these devices.

The expectation of mobile compliance has risen so quickly, even the most well-resourced companies are having trouble keeping pace. And yet the more things change, the more they stay the same. While traditional media outlets such as newspapers, TV, radio and billboards are all feeling the gravity of digital, their legacy products are still relevant when it comes to driving awareness, interest and customers to your business. What's changed is that your customers' path to purchase now includes a pit stop to check out your online presence. Word of mouth has gone viral, where one bad apple can potentially spoil a whole orchard. Trying to hide from it is to hide from your customers, giving your rivals a competitive edge that you can't afford to give up.

Overwhelming? You bet. But getting out of your comfort zone and meeting your customers where they are is what successful business growth is all about. The same resources that your customers are already using to educate themselves about you can become your greatest ally. Over the next several chapters we will walk through the importance of having a website that's uniquely yours, how to put your best foot forward when it comes to being found online, how to get a handle on social media without losing control of the conversation and touch on some of the current best practices related to marketing your business online. Finally, we'll gaze into the crystal ball and try to predict what's next for the Internet.

Action Items

1) Assess your digital presence
2) Start talking to your customers about their online habits
3) Be open to new ways of thinking

Chapter 2
Your Website

"The Internet is becoming the town square for the global village of tomorrow." - Bill Gates

Having a website to represent your brand online is no longer optional. It has become as (if not more) vital to your success as electricity itself. Your website also represents something very special, as it is the only thing that you can ever take ownership of online. There will never be a more definitive source on the topic of your business than your own website. Although there are many do-it-yourself options for creating your own website, just like you most-likely hired professionals to build your storefront and create your marketing materials, hiring a reputable firm to create your customer's first impression is worth more than a moment of consideration.

Regardless of whether you hire someone else or decide to go it alone, it is critically important that your website has three features. First, easily accessible points of conversion (phone numbers, contact forms, etc.) need to be featured predominantly throughout your site. The more clicks you put between your customers and the information they are looking for represent more reasons for them to do business with someone else. Second, your website **must** be able to recognize what type of device it is being loaded on and respond accordingly. Customers have an unbelievably short attention span, and unless your website gives them a good user experience they will impulsively seek out an alternative. Finally, search engines hate duplicate content (for reasons we will get into in the next chapter). That is why it is critical that whoever is creating your site is doing so with fresh, original content that is not copied from another website (industry-specific development companies are notorious for doing this).

Remember the days when websites proudly told you that you were visitor 00000327? The same technology used back then to track website visits has evolved as well. Nowadays, Google offers free code called 'Google Analytics' that any web developer (or even you, with a little effort) can add to your website. This code allows you to not only see how many people are coming to your website, but even what is bringing them there. There are a ton of resources online for how best to utilize this information to your advantage. Regardless, if you keep your website a secret by not promoting it online, in your store, on your business cards or anywhere else you display information about your products or services, the chances of customers finding you are slim. Building a website without a promotional strategy is like building a house without a driveway. You've worked so hard to get your business off the ground... don't keep it a secret!

Action Items

4) Make sure your site is mobile friendly
5) Keep your content unique
6) Add Google tracking code

Chapter 3
Search Engines

*"As long as one keeps searching,
the answers come."* ~ Joan Baez

Google was founded on a single guiding
principle: "Organize the world's information
and make it universally accessible and useful."
I wonder if when they crafted that statement in
the late 90s they had any idea just how much
information the world actually contained! You
might be more familiar with Yahoo, Bing, AOL
or any of the other multitude of search engines
available online today, but Google has found
itself leaps and bounds above the rest, so much
so that it's even become a verb (to be fair, you
aren't technically 'Googling' something if you
aren't using Google).

More recently, as search has gone mobile,
Google has noticed a trend in how and when
people are searching. As we live in a
distracting world, people have generally taken
to seeking information in stolen moments
throughout the day (in line for a latte, waiting
for a bus). Google started referring to these as
'micro-moments,' and has gone to great lengths
to ensure that search customers have a good

user experience with their platform. Remember that phone-friendly website we talked about in Chapter 2? This is where the rubber meets the road. With 126,000 sites to choose from, to which website would you give preferential treatment? My guess would be the one that gave your users a good experience.

Search engines care about one thing... relevance. It is impossible to engage a search engine without asking a question (even if you don't state it as such). It is then the search engine's responsibility to get you the most relevant answer to your question as quickly as possible. And quickly is quite an understatement. The average list of results is curated in less than one second, and often contains tens of thousands of potential answers to the question posed. In fact, if you are on Google's results page for longer than a few seconds, they make note of that and consider it a failure of service to you, their customer. Think of it like this: If you wanted a pizza and got results related to hardware stores, how long would you keep relying on that company as a resource? Not long at all.

Knowing that relevancy is key, there are three ways that a business can show up on a results page. We will review each component individually, but generally speaking the more real estate you can capture on a results page the more likely someone will choose you as the answer to the question they are asking. Additionally, any company that promises they can get you to the top spot with any consistency is, in a word... lying. Google changes their formula more than 500 times each year (that's on average more than once per day). They are in a constant battle with companies and individuals trying to clamor to the top of the heap, regardless of relevancy.

The strategy of any (reputable) firm is to simply get you more exposure to people who have already indicated they have a need for your product or service. In fact, Google even has a preferred vendor list of companies that they believe are acting in the best interest of their customers. It's important to note that almost anyone can call themselves a 'representative' or 'certified partner' of Google, but as of the time of this publication less than three dozen firms worldwide have been given the distinction of 'premier partner.' For a complete list of current vendors, do a search on Google for 'Premier SMB Partner List.' It's also important to remember that these premium services, as expected, come at a bit of a premium price. Only you can decide which path is right for your business and your budget.

The first (and most reliable) way to show up on a results page is to pay for the space. Whether you do it yourself, through a premier partner, or via your cousin's best friend's son, the recommended budget is dictated by the free market. Specifically, it is a strategic formula based primarily on how many people are actively looking for your services in that area and what your competitors are willing to pay to capture that lead. This means that paying more doesn't necessarily force your ad into a better position, and that under-budgeting your campaign can actually hurt you in the long run.

Another important thing to remember is that, as with anything in life, you get what you pay for. Smaller budgets mean fewer clicks, fewer calls and less overall traction for your campaign. This could lead to lackluster results and the feeling that you really 'didn't get anything' for your investment, when in actuality you got exactly what you paid for: minimum coverage.

Remember, search engines primarily care about relevancy. If you only show up once in awhile, you are identified as being 'less relevant,' and subsequently could be charged *more* than another business that shows up consistently. Comparably, if you insist on showing up for less-than-relevant searches (or, notably, when someone searches for your competitor's brand name), you run the risk of being penalized for your actions. And once you are identified as someone who doesn't play by the rules, it becomes very, very difficult to rebuild that trust.

It's also important to note that it's always free to be seen. You're not actually charged for the ad until someone clicks on it. So, unlike most ads that act as a vacuum for leads, think of your paid search ad as more of a filter, designed to keep out as many non-relevant searchers as possible. One final note on paid search ads: resist the urge to search for yourself! Search engines have an annoying habit of tracking every action (and nonaction), so repeatedly searching for your ad (and then not clicking it) only teaches the search engine that your ad is not relevant to whatever question you just asked.

The second way to show up in a results page is to get yourself listed in the search engine's map listing. The process varies from site to site, but they all traditionally have some basic information to start. From there, you go through a fairly simple process of claiming your listing by verifying that you are the business owner, usually via a phone call to the business. Once verified, you will have the opportunity to update all of your information, add photos and respond to any user feedback left by your customers. Changes are usually processed and updated within a week, but depending on how many other businesses do what you do in the area, you may or may not show up when someone searches for "Find XYZ services near me." The device knows where it is (more-or-less), so searches like this are frequent. Accurate name, address and phone records (NAP, for short) are also crucial in helping out the remaining way to show up.

The final option for showing up on a results page is perhaps the most complex yet fundamentally basic way to be found: Be so relevant to the question that you are one of the first ten freely ranked websites out of the tens (and sometimes hundreds) of thousands of results. In another book, you might see a strategy supporting this natural selection defined as 'Search Engine Optimization,' or 'SEO' for short.[4] A comprehensive and successful search strategy takes into account factors both on your site, as well as other sources on the Internet that can link back to your site. YouTube, as it so happens, is owned by Google. Therefore, any relevant content that resides on YouTube that connects back to your website will instantly give you more credibility.

When it comes to credibility, John Carcutt, an industry leader in search engine strategy, says that it really comes down to three things: Authority, Relevancy and Trust (ART). To be seen as an authority on a topic, you must have frequent updates that are relevant to whatever the searcher is looking for. Doing this with frequency, while playing by the rules, will help you build trust. The more you build your ART, the better your relationship with the search engines will be and the better your chances of being ranked higher on a search results page.

---

[4] *In an otherwise jargon-free book, I've taken the liberty of defining this one term specifically because it is so heavily used and abused in the industry. It would be a disservice to you, the reader, to not identify it properly.*

When it comes to search engines, the target is constantly moving. Ultimately, anything that you do to invest in your own website will help, but be wary of taking your foot off the gas. One of the great myths is that you 'drop' in position if you don't update your site for a while. As they say, even if you're on the right track -- if you don't move eventually you will get run over.

Action Items

    7) Claim your free map listings
    8) Seek out trusted advisors
    9) Never stop moving forward

Chapter 4
Directories & Reviews

"If you fuel your journey on the opinions
of others, you will quickly run out of gas."
~ Dr. Steve Maraboli

They say if you don't have anything nice to say then don't say anything at all. Generally speaking, the Internet is unfamiliar with this expression. In the good ol' days, a happy customer would tell a few people that he or she had a positive experience with your business. An unhappy customer would tell a few more. Today, that happy customer still tells only a few people about the experience, but the unhappy customer tells the world.

From Google to Yelp, YP (formerly Yellow Pages) to Angie's List and TripAdvisor, there are countless sites available on the Internet for disgruntled guests (or employees) to air their grievances in the court of public opinion. And with 88% of consumers trusting online reviews as much as personal recommendations,[5] to follow the ostrich and bury your head in the sand is to lull yourself into a false sense of

---

[5] BrightLocal Local Consumer Review Survey 2014.

security. In fact, the only thing worse than not saying anything at all is to try and publicly defend yourself and your business.

Think about the last time you came across bad service. What would leave you with a better brand impression: A manager explaining why their employee was right and why you were wrong, or a simple apology with an attempt to right the wrong you **felt** in that moment?

When it comes down to it, I've come to realize that the vast majority of online conflict stems from either miscommunication or misunderstanding of the attempted communication. The other major source of fuel to the fire comes in the form of what's referred to as "keyboard confidence." In other words, you'd type things that you'd never say when shrouded in the anonymity of the Internet. Well, you wouldn't... but many people do.

So how do you handle a bad review? The first step is to allow the emotional, defensive, knee-jerk reaction wash over you while your hands are anywhere but resting on the keyboard. The time to be indignant and the time to repair a customer relationship are mutually exclusive. Only after your emotions have stabilized may you start to formulate a measured response.

It is also worth noting that until you get the hang of this, it may take two or three attempts before you are able to maintain your composure through the entire response. You owe it to your client, your business, and most importantly yourself to adhere to this process until you have successfully filtered out any personal bias.

Numerous studies cite the benefits of responding with sympathetic but neutral language when it comes to boosting your business image online. The best response is the one you would give to an irate customer at your counter as your other customers waited with anticipation to observe your reaction.

The only exception to this rule is when it becomes necessary to correct objectively incorrect information that threatens more than just your ego. False statements regarding the safety of your product need to be dealt with in the same fashion as subjective remarks, but with supplemental facts that serve to defend your product. There is a significant difference between "your product sucks" and "your product injured me." Learn this difference.

As with many things in life, the best defense is often a good offense. Almost every directory allows a verified business owner to update and enhance their stock business profile for free. This also serves a dual-purpose in assisting the directory in their effort to be more accurate (and more relevant).

For known issues where negative backlash is expected, proactively publishing a press release on your website will give you a much-needed resource to which to refer angry customers within the context of the review. This not only makes you look better overall, but you may be able to stop a bad situation from becoming worse.

Despite all the negativity, every once in a great while a customer has such a great experience that they feel compelled to share it with the Internet. These brave souls should be praised with all of the enthusiasm you can manage. Nothing wins the hearts and minds of the general public faster than consistently prompt, measured responses from a business.

When it comes to online directories and reviews, getting ahead of inaccurate information and maintaining composure in the face of overwhelming negativity is the key to survival. If you can master these elements you will set yourself up for success, and you may even help an unhappy customer in the process.

Action Items

10) Always be positive
11) Update inaccurate info
12) Control the conversation

Chapter 5
Social Media

"Marketing is no longer about the stuff
you make, but about the stories you tell."
~ Seth Godin

I still remember getting an invite from my friend Jess for this new social network called, "The Facebook." I already had established a MySpace page, so at the time I didn't really feel the need for another online profile, but Jess promised me that this was somehow different. Plus I felt like I was being invited into an exclusive club, as up until that point only Ivy League schools such as my friend's alma mater, Dartmouth, could gain access.

Flash forward just over a decade and the social network now known just as "Facebook" boasts over **one billion** users (that's 1/7th of the planet, for those playing along at home). Running alongside and gaining in popularity include familiar names such as Twitter and LinkedIn, as well as some newer players such as Vine, Instagram, Pinterest, Periscope and Snapchat.

Social media has become the new word of mouth and, much like directories and review sites, one bad apple can ruin your reputation in 140 characters or less. Each platform has its own primary function and its own language, of sorts. Fortunately, each social service also helps new users become acquainted with the landscape through guides, tutorials and walkthroughs. At their heart, however, these networks, much like humans, are social (hence the term 'social' media).

Social media is alluring in that most of the base services are offered at no cost, but buyer beware, this does not make them 'free,' unless of course your time is also worth nothing. Time spent sharing content online is time not spent in other areas of your business. It turns out time really does equal money, and that's not all. These networks are for-profit companies, which means they will do their part to separate you from your money. This includes tactics like suppressing the exposure of your content and then charging you to strategically 'boost' that exposure back to normal levels. The benefit here is that, thanks to self-disclosure, you can target these ads very effectively, but it still falls under the umbrella of 'sponsored content.'

Entire books have been dedicated to the intricacies of each social network, but as this book is designed to be a primer for small business owners, I am going to focus this chapter primarily on the two most-utilized networks for small business: Facebook and Twitter. It is also worth mentioning that Instagram (a photo-sharing platform) is owned by Facebook and that Vine and Periscope (video sharing services) are owned by Twitter.

There are three different classifications of profiles on Facebook, and each represents a different classification of user. The first, personal profiles, is designed to be used exclusively for real individuals with real identities. To that end, Facebook recently started cracking down on profiles with questionable names, forcing businesses into the right category and forcing people with unique names to go to great lengths to preserve their online presence. The second classification is groups, designed exclusively for a 'group' of people to communicate regarding a common topic or interest. Groups can be either exclusive or public, and participants generally frown on any off-topic conversation.

The final classification of profile is what is known as a page. These pages have been specifically designed for a public business or entity to invite people to 'like' them on Facebook (as opposed to joining groups and requesting or adding friends). Once you've created a page, you can invite people to like your page either online or offline by way of in-store signage and casual conversation. Some businesses will also celebrate milestone attendance to their page by awarding prizes to the 100th or 1000th person to like their page.

On Facebook, you post content to your wall that you think your fans (people who have liked your page) would be interested in seeing. The key here is to strike the balance between being informative, informational and entertaining. There is no hard and fast rule as to how much you should delve into each category. The goal should be to develop a voice that is consistent and unique to your brand. Remember, this site was built on social interaction, so posing questions and being professionally playful with your fans is acceptable. It is also acceptable to post content that is relevant to your fans interests but not necessarily your brand.

Once you post anything, it is immediately and irrecoverably available for anyone on the Internet to see. Though initially only your fans may be exposed to the message, posts of questionable content have a way of finding their way off your page and into other places on the Internet such as blogs and news articles. This is why you must always follow the Golden Rule: "Think twice, publish once."

Your fans have three options when it comes to interacting with your post. They can like it to show their support (and at the time of publication, Facebook was also testing some other styles of expressive responses), share it to their personal page with the intent of broadcasting it to their network of connections, or leave a comment. Many users will combine all three actions, first liking a post and then sharing the post with their own commentary attached.

When it comes to the comments, as well as questions posed directly to your page, it is imperative that you follow the same rules as directories and reviews: prompt responses that are non-inflammatory in nature. Anything less and the Internet will come to the defense of the original poster, right or wrong. It is also crucial that you walk into this world with a tough skin.

No matter what your intention was when posting the content online someone, somewhere will misinterpret your intention and take offense to whatever you have just posted. Remain consistent, vigilant and positive. You will lose a few battles along the way, but if you stick to your guiding principles you will ultimately win the war (and the business).

Twitter was born from a desire to capture the moments between Facebook posts and has evolved (as most things online do) to a real-time information platform, essential in the reporting (and sometimes creating) of breaking news stories, as well as a term that's become known as 'Real-Time Marketing.'

When created spontaneously, Real-Time Marketing has its place, but few have the resources and creative prowess to pull it off effectively. One case study in perfect timing came during the 47th edition of a very popular football game (the name of which, incidentally, is trademarked and cannot be used in your ads, or this book, without paying the NFL).

Brands have been using Twitter as a platform for their ads since its inception in 2006, but when a power outage briefly interrupted gameplay, one advertising agency saw an opportunity to shine. 360i, the agency responsible for marketing Oreo cookies, instantly whipped up a small ad featuring a dimly lit cookie that stated, 'Power out? No problem. You can still dunk in the dark." That one message was interacted with over 20,000 times in a matter of hours (and also gained the agency several awards and honorable mentions). It's no coincidence that, since then, brands worldwide have been trying to have 'an Oreo moment.'

On Twitter, tweets (as they're called) are limited to 140 characters including spaces. Links are automatically shortened to save space and images take up their fair share of characters as well. Users can interact with your tweet by liking/favoriting[6] your tweet to show their support, retweeting it to share it with their connections or replying to it to add their commentary. As with Facebook, many users will use a combination of these interactions.

One other feature is something called a Direct Message, wherein two users that follow each other can send private messages (just like on

---

[6] For years, Twitter used the term 'Favorite' to describe the action of liking a post. They later changed this interaction to the industry standard of 'Like.'

Facebook). The key difference between the two platforms is that on Twitter all profiles are created equal, but user names may or may not be verified as the actual person they claim to be. This has led to many parody accounts being created on Twitter.

Topics of information are clustered together via the symbol '#' which has been dubbed a 'hashtag.' Once enough people use a certain hashtag, that topic becomes 'trending.' More advanced tools allow users to see what is trending either nationally or closer to home. Interestingly enough a practice known as 'hashtag hijacking' has become increasingly popular, in which a user references a hashtag for a trending topic with content that is unrelated to the topic being discussed.

To interact with other users on Facebook or Twitter, users will invoke what's referred to as the 'at' symbol (@) followed by the user's Twitter username or real name on Facebook. It is important to note that users can also use this symbol to make a reference (positive or otherwise) to your business page or Twitter account. Understanding how to respond to these interactions is vital to your success on the platform.

Regardless of whether you choose to start with Facebook or Twitter, the best recommendation is to first become an observer. Learn how others are using the service and become familiar with what your competition is doing as well. Once you learn the basics, the rest becomes easy and, if you're lucky, maybe even enjoyable!

We have now entered what is commonly referred to as the engagement or experience economy, where some would rather invest money in experiences than putting forth the effort themselves. This desire to be engaged with the brands that we buy from feeds right into the social media playbook.

Society's addiction to social media has also created some offline conditions including one affliction called "FOMO," or the fear of missing out. Numerous people (including myself) have also reported feeling "phantom vibrations," where you reflexively respond to an incoming notification you felt on your phone that didn't actually happen.

One final note on social media. To those detractors who think they can hide from technology by insisting "their customers aren't on social media," I offer two pieces of advice. First, unless you are polling your customers at the door as to their personal consumption habits, you can't be sure, and more importantly, if they truly aren't then you are missing a massive opportunity to gain market share by communicating with this underserved market... or maybe you'd rather let them buy from your competitors instead.

Action Items

13) Develop your voice
14) Don't be too promotional
15) Be proactive

Chapter 6
Banner Ads

"The man who stops advertising to save money is like the man who stops the clock to save time." ~ Henry Ford

7

On October 27th, 1994, telecommunications powerhouse AT&T purchased the first commercially available banner ad on the Internet. Since then, banner ads have become an ever-present, sometimes annoying sidekick to the free content that we all have come to expect from this environment.

Banner ads have gotten a bad rap over the years, serving predominantly as virtual billboards to the information superhighway that is the World Wide Web. While few users will ever publicly admit that they intentionally clicked on a banner ad, brands that rely on them continue to expect consumer behavior to somehow be magically transformed when

---

[7] Image Credit: TheFirstBannerAd.com

their creative message dances across the screen.

There are primarily three different ways banner ads can be purchased, and a number of different methods for getting those ads in front of the 'right' people. When it comes to buying these ads, it's important to understand exactly what you are buying and exactly what to expect. Static or fixed position ads remain locked to the same spot on the same page every time someone goes to that particular page. For those of you who insist on seeing your ad in action, this is the option for you. The other options include what's commonly referred to as a share of voice, where a percentage of a particular spot's availability is sold to multiple advertisers, or the most common option: impression-based ads.

Each time your ad is displayed online it counts as one impression. Impression-based ads are shown either on one site or a network of sites. When you purchase ads of this style, it is vital to know going in that you will most likely *never see your ad*. This does not mean, however, that the ad is not working for you. Purchasing ads in this fashion means that you know ahead of time how many times someone has the opportunity to be exposed to your business.

The win is the exposure. I cannot emphasize this point enough. Clicks, which come from highly engaged potential customers who happened to be in the market for your product or service at the exact moment they saw your ad, are purely a bonus.

The good news is there are steps that you can take to increase the likelihood of a click. First, the more content (clutter) you put in your ad, the less likely someone is to click. This could be because you gave them all the information they needed, thus eliminating the need for a click to take place, or there was too much 'noise' and the user just tuned the ad out. This is known in the industry as ad-blindness. Things like your address, phone number and fine print have no place in your banner ad. If the message is strong, they will find you.

Much like their cross-country cousin the billboard, the goal of a banner ad should be to create enough curiosity in those precious few seconds of exposure and leave, well, an impression. Generally speaking, businesses that utilize this method of advertising tend to see a boost in website traffic more often from the search engines than the ads themselves. If the ad is doing its job right, the user will remember enough of it to conduct a search at a later point. And, if you've been reading this book sequentially, you already know what they'll find.

The second thing you can do to give your campaign the best chance for success is target the right audience. Advertising reps have historically targeted based on demographics (women 25-54, men 18-49, etc.) and psychographics (people's interests and hobbies). Recently, a handful of companies have started capitalizing on all of the data that is readily available in the market to fine-tune this process even more.

Over time, your computer gets to know you based on what you search for, where you browse to and what you purchase. Based on this information, your computer then builds an (anonymous) profile based on your personal habits... but it doesn't stop there. Remember when you registered for that loyalty card at your favorite grocery store? I bet you gave them your email address so they could send you coupons relevant to your shopping experience. Now your computer can tie this data into what it already knows about your online habits. It all sounds very Big Brother until you realize that all this effort is made to show you more relevant ads that you are more likely to interact and engage with. Companies that are using this information tend to target people's online interest and intentions rather than specific sites. And until something new comes along, this is the most targeted advertising money can buy.

The final thing you can do to increase clicks to your ad is to 'retarget' your ads to people who have already been on your website or have previously seen your ad. This is done through a small bit of code that can be fairly easily installed by the person who created your website. You've no doubt seen this code in action if you've ever researched something online. While it may be perceived as intrusive, business owners love it because there is zero waste.

Banner ads, much like any other form of advertising, take time and money to work and show their effectiveness. Stay creative, stay consistent and, with the right expectations, banner ads can be an effective weapon in your arsenal of advertising.

Action Items

16) Target people, not sites
17) Set realistic goals
18) Think creatively

Chapter 7
Email Marketing

"Nobody reads ads. People read what interests them. Sometimes it's an ad."
~ Howard Gossage

Like many other things in the digital world, email communication has evolved over time. In its early days, it was used primarily for office communication. When AOL rose to popularity in the late 90s, the phrase "You've Got Mail" became the catchphrase of the Internet (so much so, that Tom Hanks and Meg Ryan co-starred in a romantic movie of the same title).

Along with digital greeting cards and family messages, another staple of the American inbox was spam. These unsolicited messages ran rampant until 2003 when the US government passed the CAN-SPAM Act which, for the first time, established national guidelines surrounding email communication. It didn't stop the problem, but it certainly helped to curb the volume of spam messages being sent.

It was around this time that email became popular enough for companies and businesses to start offering incentives for you to share your email address with them. Once these lists became large enough, email then became a critical marketing tool which is still effectively used today.

Today's email marketer has access to data of which business owners could only dream. While there are a wide variety of programs that have the ability to manage the distribution of your email communication, almost all of them have the ability to tell you how many people opened, interacted with, and even unsubscribed from your message.

It is critically important to respect the wishes of someone who has unsubscribed from your list, as not doing so would be a violation of the CAN-SPAM Act and could get you in trouble with the law. Comparatively, Canada's Anti-Spam Law (CASL) carries a fine of up to ten million dollars for businesses that are non-compliant. Virtually every email program will include an opt-out option and unsubscribe someone from your email database automatically completely at the user's request.
So how can you use email to your benefit? Start by giving your customers an opportunity to provide their email address, and maybe a few more pieces of critical demographic information. The more you ask them to

disclose, however, the less likely they will be to opt-in. You may also consider offering something in return, such as a coupon or voucher, to incentivize the customer to take action.

Once you establish a list of email addresses, you can import this information into an email marketing program of your preference. They all have different features and most offer the opportunity to purchase a bank of credits, deducting from your balance each time you send an email. Another nice feature of many of these programs are pre-made templates that allow you to 'drag and drop' your content with ease.

Once you have everything ready, I always recommend sending a test message to either yourself or a small group of trusted individuals to make sure that everything looks right (and is spelled correctly). From there, you are free to unleash your message to the world (or at least the part of the world that has given you permission to send them email).

The content of your message should be promotional in nature, with strong calls-to-action throughout. Be careful, however, on being too enthusiastic. Overly-hyped language, too many exclamation points and especially the word 'free' (in the subject line or content of the message) all tend to put spam blocking software on alert. You also want to try and strike a balance between text and imagery, as messages that are too far in either direction might never see the intended inbox.

The final thought on email marketing is to use it sparingly. People get a lot of email and, unless you have a really compelling reason, you really shouldn't have a need to email your customers more than once a month. Stick with these guidelines, and you'll be one step closer to bringing a customer back through your door.

Action Items

19) Always ask for email addresses
20) Respect the unsubscriber
21) Don't overdo it

Chapter 8
What's Next?

*"The best way to predict your future
is to create it." ~ Abraham Lincoln*

The digital landscape is ever changing, and keeping up with the Internet is equivalent to chasing a sunset. As technology and platforms continue to evolve, even the brightest minds in the space can't say with 100% certainty what could be lurking around the next corner.

For my part, I personally believe that augmented reality will be the next 'new normal' for our society. Be it visors, headbands, microchips or even digital contact lenses, we're already seeing virtual reality making inroads and it's only a matter of time before this technology too takes center stage.

Technology has always come with benefits and risks, but as our society acclimates to what, just a few years ago was identified as impossible, I think the positive will continue to outweigh and outshine the negative.

Those that survive the digital revolution we are living through will be those that were light on their feet and easily adaptive to constant change. The good news is the very thing that is creating the problem is also providing the solution, if you know where to look. Interwoven into the pages of the Internet itself is a definitive guide on how to use it.

If you're not yet comfortable seeking answers from the source, local resources such as your nearest library or chamber of commerce can provide a treasure trove of information.

Another option is to look to your industry leaders for best practices. After all, the best way to learn is from other people's mistakes. Staying committed to learning will be the key to your success and, if all else fails, just ask Google.

Action Items

22)Commit to learning
23)Utilize local resources
24)Follow the leader

25 Action Steps Review

1) Assess your digital presence
2) Start talking to your customers about their online habits
3) Be open to new ways of thinking
4) Make sure your site is mobile friendly
5) Keep your content unique
6) Add Google tracking code
7) Claim your free map listings
8) Seek out trusted advisors
9) Never stop moving forward
10) Always be positive
11) Update inaccurate info
12) Control the conversation
13) Develop your voice
14) Don't be too promotional
15) Be proactive
16) Target people, not sites
17) Set realistic goals
18) Think creatively
19) Always ask for email addresses
20) Respect the unsubscriber
21) Don't overdo it
22) Commit to learning
23) Utilize local resources
24) Follow the leader
25) Have Fun!

About The Author

Brandon Tidd is a native of Cleveland, Ohio. He graduated with honors from Kent State University before pursuing a career in sales. For more than a decade Brandon has been a champion of small business, having worked for some of the largest media and tech companies in the world including CBS and AOL. He founded his own website development firm in 2005, personally helping over 150 small businesses establish their first presence on the Internet. When he's not in front of a computer, Brandon enjoys spending time with his wife and two cats, DJing private events and volunteering on the Cuyahoga Valley Scenic Railroad.

www.ingramcontent.com/pod-product-compliance
Lightning Source LLC
Chambersburg PA
CBHW021444170526
45164CB00001B/386